CHAOS TO PEACE

HOPE AND DIRECTION FOR THE FRUSTRATED PARENT

BRETT QUANTRILLE
Licensed Clinical Social Worker

The information contained herein is for educational purposes only. It is not intended as a substitute for the diagnosis, treatment, or advice by a qualified licensed professional. A conscious effort has been made to only present information that is both accurate and truthful. I assume no responsibility for how this material is used or for any errors, inaccuracies, omissions, or inconsistency herein. All names and situations used in examples are fictitious. Any slights of people or organizations are unintentional.

From Chaos to Peace: Hope and Direction for the Frustrated Parent

Copyright © 2014 by Brett Quantrille.

All rights reserved. No part of this book may be modified, reproduced, or transmitted in any form or by any means, electronic or mechanical, including emailing, photocopying, recording, or otherwise without the prior written permission of the publisher.

Published by Inspired Publishing, LLC

Author Photo by Melissa Foshee

Illustrations by Marketa Gautreaux

Cover Design by Rodellwahrin A. Pepito

Edited by Lorraine Fico-White, Magnifico Manuscripts, LLC

Book Design and Layout by Lorie DeWorken, MIND*the*MARGINS, LLC

ISBN-10: 0-9905757-0-5
ISBN-13: 978-0-9905757-0-2

Praise for *From Chaos to Peace*

Excellent. This book is a quick read that is full of actionable items that will enable any family to quickly develop a game plan to truly move from Chaos to Peace. Great read!

Kyle Dean, MD

As a practicing pediatrician, I often see families desperate for direction in parenting. *From Chaos to Peace* offers parents practical methods for achieving a happy home life. Say good-bye to yelling and frustration and chaos. Say hello to peace!

Jennifer T. Guidroz, MD, FAAP

From Chaos to Peace provides needed hope and suggestions for families in crisis. The author shares practical ideas and a workable plan to manage difficulties in the home through consistency, structure, routine, and discipline. This book will be an encouragement to parents of children of all ages.

Joseph L. Palotta, MD
Board Certified Psychiatrist

Mr. Quantrille's book is an easy-to-follow how-to guide that can begin to strengthen families almost immediately! His focus on the importance of strengthening the parent(s) leadership role in order to achieve family equilibrium is key and often downplayed or even overlooked in like parenting books. *From Chaos to Peace* also effectively addresses single parent households or homes with only "one determined parent." Having worked with families and children myself for over 20 years, I truly believe that *From Chaos to Peace* has the great potential to benefit our society as a whole, one family at a time!

Michael J. Sunseri, LCSW
Licensed Clinical Social Worker

Dedication

I dedicate this book to my beautiful wife, Debbie, and our two children, Duncan and Isabel. I am so blessed to have you as family. Thank you so very much, Deb, for the unconditional love you give us on a daily basis. You are the kindest person I know.

Kiddies, words cannot express how very grateful and honored I am to be your daddy. I'm so very proud of the responsible young adults you are growing up to be.

Thank you for the patience and prayers during this tremendous process. I love you.

Acknowledgments

I want to thank my friends, some of over 40 years, who have remained loyal through thick and thin. I want to thank my colleagues, especially the study group, who has been a tremendous blessing to me. And as for my family, words cannot adequately express how much you mean to me. Thank you all, each and every one, for your support.

*If you want a well-behaved child,
you first have to become a calm leader.
Peace begins with you.*

Table of Contents

Parent to Parent xi

PART 1
Parenting with Warmth and Firmness 3

Chapter 1: Today Chaos, Tomorrow Peace 5

Chapter 2: Steps to Peaceful Living 15

Chapter 3: Transforming the Attitudes 31

Chapter 4: Improving Parenting Skills 39

PART 2
Creating and Implementing The Family Check System 45

Chapter 5: Leading and Guiding with Purpose 47

Chapter 6: Routine Planning 55

Chapter 7: Discipline Planning 69

Chapter 8: Reward Planning 93

Conclusion 109

Appendix 113

Parent to Parent

*Patience and empathy
are keys to all healthy relationships.*

Dear Parent,

I am a licensed clinical social worker, and I have devoted my life to the well-being of children. I have worked in outpatient and inpatient facilities, crisis-oriented settings such as the emergency room, schools, group homes, and both juvenile and adult detention centers. In the last few years alone, I have treated hundreds of children, adolescents and families in my private practice, assisting them in improving various life areas and conditions.

In time, I came to realize that, to help children, I needed to help their parents. With this in mind, I developed *From Chaos to Peace*, a program to teach parents how to manage difficult, non-compliant children and reconnect with them emotionally to bring balance and love back to the relationship.

This program evolved many years ago. I, too, lived in a chaotic household. Parenting was poor, and my marriage was in distress. Our children had too much power, and we were responsible. We realized that to turn the tide we had to learn how to discipline our children, provide consistency and structure, and nurture them so we could all connect on an emotional level. Also, we needed to set an example and not undermine each other's authority. If we didn't respect each other, how could our children respect us?

I studied much and over the years developed the successful program outlined in this book. *From Chaos to Peace* not only took our family from chaos to peace but numerous other families as well. It can for your family, also. In this book, you will learn the approaches and skills to help you achieve peace. In time, you will transform the nature of your relationship with your child from one of conflict to one of peace, cooperation, mutual respect, quality, and enjoyment. It matters not if the constant power struggles occur because your child is difficult or oppositional because of temperament, learning disabilities, or emotional problems. The *From Chaos to Peace (FC2P) Program* helps turn the turbulent tide for children. All that is required is your determination and willingness to follow my program with an open mind and heart and to implement it consistently.

Once you learn to parent authoritatively, you will discover how to appropriately connect with your child. When you achieve this, your child will give you the respect back and develop into an effective, healthy, and functional teenager and young adult!

In peace,
Brett Quantrille, LCSW
Licensed Clinical Social Worker

PART 1

Parenting with Warmth and Firmness

Chapter 1

Today Chaos, Tomorrow Peace

*Peace begins with good insights into parenting,
appropriate responses to our children,
and good leadership.*

Have you ever felt so frustrated with your child that you lost your temper and screamed piercing words? Most parents have, either from something that happens at home, like the child not doing chores, or at school, perhaps the child is defiant and refuses to follow directions.

Likewise, you've probably lost your temper at some point with your spouse. Perhaps you feel overloaded with responsibilities and chores and feel overwhelmed because it's not being shared. Or perhaps your spouse refuses to set limits and discipline the children and you fight about this.

These are all common events in families that get resolved for the most part. But in some families, such chaos is the modus operandi and constant tension exists in the home. Everyone is at each other, and worst of all, your family has become disconnected emotionally and disengaged. You constantly lock horns about everything—doing chores, doing homework, mistreating siblings, what to eat, what to wear. This sparks a flame and you lose your temper. Your child disrespects you by back-talking and this leads to a shouting match. Your child wins because you "lost it." And the cycle continues and occurs more often and with greater intensity.

Moreover, the school phones frequently with negative reports about your child. Every time the phone rings you cringe or almost panic because your child has an unresolved behavior problem, and you haven't as of yet found approaches and strategies that will help him. (Note: The singular gender "he" will be used throughout the book to represent either gender and can also pertain to multiple children). The tension and drama have become unbearable, and you desperately need relief.

Many reasons exist for such chaos. Life stressors that are unwanted, and life choices that are voluntary can be sources. Illness, too much responsibility, and lack of parental insight can all be triggers. Or simply having a difficult, hard-to-manage disobedient and disrespectful child who sadly brings out the worst in you can be the trigger for the chaos in your family.

Typical Example: The Eversley Family

The family consists of the father (a paramedic), the mother (a preschool teacher), and three children: thirteen-year-old Timothy, seven-year-old Ian, and six-year-old Cassie. They live in a bungalow in a close-knit neighborhood and attend church regularly.

Like many families today, they felt stressed to the max. The children were disrespectful and defiant. Timothy back-talked all the time and constantly lost phone privileges, which made him furious. Cassie lied and refused to comply with her parents' demands like cleaning her room or picking up her dirty dishes. Ian was explosive and anxious, constantly throwing temper tantrums. Mom, who felt disorganized and was on anti-depressive medicine, reacted to the kids' disruptive behavior by yelling and ultimately giving in. Meanwhile, Dad had no patience for their bad behavior and tended to hit them and punish them with severe restrictions.

Mom and Dad came to see me hoping that my *From Chaos to Peace (FC2P) Program* would help them manage their children better, especially Ian who was in second grade. Ian cried a lot, worried much, and was often angry and frustrated. He was disruptive at home and very stubborn when he didn't get his way, quickly throwing a temper tantrum. If Dad was home, he would scream at Ian and spank him, while Mom gave in. Consequently, the parenting was inconsistent and the two parents argued frequently, creating more stress and marital problems and increasing Ian's anxiety and anger. Ian described his parents as his father "not saying a lot" and his mother "not caring what I do."

Problems also existed regarding school. Ian was mildly bullied by his peers and for that reason often complained he felt sick and didn't want to go to school. He especially disliked going to in-school assemblies like talent shows since crowds made him anxious. Mother permitted him to miss school when he didn't want to go and brought him instead to her preschool, which Ian liked. If the father found out, he got furious and demanded that Ian go to school unless he was sick enough to go to a doctor. Dad insisted that Ian attend the assemblies with the rest of the kids since "being afraid of crowds is 'sissy behavior' and you have to get over it."

Fed up with the chaos in their home, both parents were completely compliant in implementing the *FC2P Program*. Mom committed to not yelling and arguing anymore with her children, which helped tremendously, while Dad worked hard to remain calm and not lose his patience. Mom spoke with the school about the kids bullying Ian, which in turn lessened. Both parents agreed Ian didn't have to attend school assemblies but in place of playing with the kids in Mom's preschool, they hired a tutor to work with Ian in the library at school on school assembly days. After six weeks on the program, Mom reported that peace in her home had increased significantly just through her not arguing anymore with her children. The parents said all three children were doing great and ended treatment with me.

Remarkably, Mom scored 250% higher on her parenting skills survey at the end of treatment compared to before treatment, while Dad had a 100% increase!

Mom said, "I learned how to discipline and how to follow through. I learned how to slow down and adjust to having children. I was in overdrive. Now I have downshifted, and by parenting at a slower pace, things are much more peaceful."

Dad stated he was skeptical about coming to therapy but today felt grateful that he did since the program ". . . organized us and brought peace to my family." The marriage has also improved as the parents are now able to have couples time in the evening whereas before they spent little time together.

Like the Eversley family, you may likely feel it's time for a more manageable household, governed by a set of rules, plans, and methods that bring and maintain peace. It doesn't matter if the problem in your family is related to "school," "parenting," "marital," "My child is *just* bad," or a combination of these. It's time for help!

A parent's responsibility is to motivate children without damaging, inspire without destroying the spirit, love and serve without overindulging, teach a work ethic without enabling irresponsibility (such as doing their work for them). Your goal is to meet your children where they are emotionally and developmentally, and help them to do their best, be responsible, and grow as a human being. You can achieve this by following the same *FC2P Program* that the Eversley family did.

Q&A

How long will the program take start to finish?
How long it will take depends on your willingness and diligence in following my program consistently with an open mind and heart. Typically, you will begin to see significant improvement in your parent/child relationship within a few weeks. Allow a few months to achieve the desired result.

How fast should I go at implementing this program?
Go at your own pace so the transition from chaos to peace doesn't feel overwhelming. You will drastically need to change the way you have been parenting and doing things and replace them with the *FC2P Program* methods and practices and this will take time.

Is the *FC2P Program* only for young children?
The program can be implemented from toddlers to teens successfully.

What if my spouse doesn't cooperate?
It only takes one determined parent to significantly improve your child's behavior.

What will be required of me as the parent?

- You will need to carry out the program consistently. If you waver and give in to your child's demands *at any point,* your child will take back control and your efforts will be for naught. The program is entirely dependent on you following through.

- You will need to make your child's character a priority—above social events of parents, social events of children, extracurricular activities of children, hobbies of parents, privileges of children, schooling for parents and children, and work of parents. In other words, if the school calls that your child has been a problem, your first priority is going to the school to get to the root of the problem regardless of other commitments. One of the most important decisions you will ever make lies in whether or not you will put the needs of your child in front of your own.

- You must be willing to stand up for your child and against the bullish or permissive parenting of your spouse.

- You must determine to bring structure to your home.

- You must be willing to solve problems with your spouse and move forward.

- You must be willing to commit and never quit on your child.

- You cannot be at any point permissive or harsh. That means you can no longer give in to your child out of fear that he won't love you anymore, or play the boss or drill sergeant to enforce control. Rather, you will take the authoritative approach to parenting by blending love, strength, respect, warmth, and firmness. Love must be unconditional and a constant, not conditional and inconsistent. Patience and love are keys to all healthy relationships. You must have the heart of a teacher.

- You need to acknowledge that you, not just your child, are responsible for the chaos. Once you begin to curb your anger or anxiety and act rationally, you will be seen as the adult in charge.

- Barring specific psychiatric or medical diagnoses beyond your control, you must take responsibility for the way your child is behaving.

What kinds of changes can I expect to see?
Parent
- You will have a basic understanding of how to create peace in your home and how to maintain it.
- You will give your child instructions in a more deliberate and loving manner.
- You will become more patient and feel calmer and more relaxed.
- You will address your child's attitude and not allow him to slide by with anything. (No eye rolling, noises, remarks, or stomping around.)
- You will learn better control of your anger and/or anxiety and no longer allow your emotions to damage your relationship with your child.
- You will no longer be permissive or harsh but will learn to be an authoritative parent.
- You and your child will fulfill basic parent and child roles more easily. Your child will honor and respect you by saying "Yes" or "Yes, ma'am" when you give directives. You will resist nagging and yelling.
- You will become a better leader, which could mean telling your child "No" more often, responding more often in a calm tone of voice, or following through with what you say you will do more of the time.

Child
- Your child will go from out of control and angry all the time to obedient and cooperative and do things when you instruct him to do so.
- Your child will learn to be polite.
- You will find that once your child learns to accept your authority, it translates to accepting other people's authority like teachers and bosses.
- Your child will grow into an independent, autonomous, successful individual.

Will the program make me more successful as a parent?

Yes, you will be more successful if you follow these guidelines:
- Love unconditionally
- Lead by example
- Be loyal
- Forgive when offended
- Set limits when necessary
- Be empathetic
- Be willing to pursue the relationship
- Communicate regularly
- Be respectful
- Be honest and trustworthy
- If your child has a problem with your behavior, be humble, talk about it, and listen to his point of view.

Chapter 2

STEPS TO PEACEFUL LIVING

*A parent's priority is to create an environment
of mutual respect and warmth,
not to condemn.*

You are now ready to start the *FC2P Program*. As you begin the program, your goal is to build successful exchanges between your child and you. This may take time. Have patience. Focus on practicing the approaches in this chapter until you achieve an acceptable level of peaceful relations in your family. Character shaping and child training will come once you finish your *Family Check System* and begin to implement and follow through with your plans.

To gain your child's respect, build your child's character, and bring peace and harmony to your household, your goal is to become an authoritative parent who sets limits, creates rules and reasonable consequences when they're not followed, and who parents warmly but firmly. To do this you will have to give up being a controlling—"my way or the highway"—or a permitting, "wishy-washy" and "whatever"—parent. A bossy, indecisive, apathetic, and otherwise disengaged or emotionally disconnected parent creates anger, fear, and insecurity in a child. To go from chaos to peace, you must lose these attitudes.

Transitioning from Controlling Parenting to Authoritative Parenting

When you parent with an aggressive or hostile approach, your children behave—but out of fear, not out of respect. And remember, your goal is mutual respect. You will also create angry, fearful children who lack confidence and will later have difficulty in forming an intimate relationship. When they become teens, they may rebel against your authority and become delinquent.

Here's how to begin to take steps to lose this parenting style:

STEP 1: Stop using "family destroyers"
A family destroyer is anything said or done in such a way that tears down or hurts the child's spirit. This includes any negative parenting such as:

- Aggressive parenting

- Bullying
- Yelling
- Screaming
- Guilt tripping
- Being overly critical
- Arguing
- Threatening
- False judging
- Condemning
- Lecturing
- Losing temper
- Using sarcasm
- Being impatient
- Silence or cold shouldering

Cease these behaviors immediately. Stop them altogether, if you can. They will not serve your purpose of creating organization, warmth, and mutual respect in your relationship with your child.

STEP 2: Give them back their privileges

If you've been using a controlling approach to parenting, you've likely meted out harsh loss of privileges, like loss of the use of electronics or being grounded indefinitely. It's the indefinite piece to this consequence that is excessive and an abuse of parental power, which creates anger, hopelessness, and resentment in your child. You will want to change this approach to one of meting out discipline that fits the infraction. As you learn how to do this, it's best to give back to your child some, if not all, of these cherished privileges during this stage of the *FC2P Program*. This will start to heal the broken parent/child relationship and spread good will. After you finish *The Family Check System*, you may use some of these confiscated goods and privileges to motivate the child in a more productive fashion.

STEP 3: Cease spankings
If you've been using spankings, you will want to cease this method for now. Remember, your goal is to create warmth and mutual respect not intimidation.

STEP 4: Stop nagging
Quit nagging your child to follow through with your instructions such as doing chores and doing their schoolwork, even if it means a messy room and poor grades. Mending your relationship with your child is at this point in the program top priority. Once this improves, other priorities such as school can be re-addressed.

> **PARENTING TIP:**
> It's important to be certain that you are being respectful to your child. Are you abrupt with him by turning off video games without warning? Do you give a two-to-three minute notice or set a timer? Do you tell him "We're leaving" and demand that he stop immediately what he's doing or do you give a "Five-to-ten minute advance notice"? Do you physically take things away or do you instruct your child to put the identified object in your hand or on the counter? Instructing your child to do a particular task will give him a chance to make the responsible, obedient choice. Try not to physically take things from your child. This is controlling and can even be dangerous with respect to teenagers.

Transitioning from Permissive Parenting to Authoritative Parenting

When you parent with a wishy-washy permissive approach, your child is in control—not you—and they disrespect you and run the household. They tend to be disorganized because they lack direction and discipline, do poorly in school, and as they think they can do whatever they want, fill up the principal's office and later, perhaps, jail cells.

If you are a permissive parent, you use the following strategies:

- Pretending you didn't see your child misbehave
- Being passive
- Begging and pleading
- Bargaining
- Bribing
- Giving in often
- Enabling or doing too much for the child
- Overindulging by giving the child too much

Here's how to begin to take steps to lose this parenting style and gain your parenting power:

STEP 1: No is no, not maybe
When you say "no" to your child, it's imperative that it does not become "maybe." The second it does, you've lost control of the situation. Remember, he is the child, and you are the grown-up, the parent . . . with all the experience, resources, authority, and knowledge! Use it.

STEP 2: Do not argue with your children
In place of arguing, say, "I'm not arguing with you" and turn away and ignore. If you speak after you have said you weren't going to, you lose

the battle. To gain your power back, be strong, and direct your child versus caving.

STEP 3: Don't ignore foolish behavior
If you are a permissive parent, you likely have ignored some of your child's foolish behavior. Vow to no longer let such behavior go unchecked and unsupervised. Let your child know if he is noisy and teach him a proper volume for the given situation. Let your child know if he is fidgety and educate him how to better channel his energy. When your child disobeys, disrespects, defies, lies, or otherwise rebels against your authority or demonstrates poor character, let him know it.

STEP 4: Teach gratefulness for every privilege and opportunity
If you have been given much and have extra in your finances for special opportunities like sporting events, vacations, etc., let it be known to your child that these opportunities are indeed "special" and "extra," not automatic. Teach your child about the value of a dollar and what it takes to earn these special opportunities. When you teach the value of a good work ethic, you will prevent your child from an entitlement mentality and from thinking rules and work do not apply to him.

Parenting Authoritatively

When you parent authoritatively, you are firm and reasonable while warm and loving. You set reasonable limits and when your child does not follow through, you enact thoughtful consequences that match the infraction. You give them your attention and interest. This establishes trust that translates into healthy relationships between a parent and a child.

Don't get disappointed if you can't get the result you want immediately. This probably won't happen until *The Family Check System* is completed. Take it easy on yourself. Give yourself permission to mess up and lose a battle or two. Focus on getting stronger by remaining calm or getting yourself to calm. Believe you can earn the control of your home, and in time, you will. Remember, the keys are consistency, structure, routine, and discipline. If you slip and lose a battle, vow to become more firm and determined in your resolve.

STEP 1: Set limits
Establish the rules in the house and the consequences for not following them. If your child starts to argue or misbehave, don't argue with them. Remind them what the rule is and the consequence. You may say: "I've given you an answer;" "No means no;" or "I've said 'no'" followed by walking away. Don't argue. Ignore your child if you need to.

STEP 2: Use discipline, not punishment
There's a big difference between punishment and discipline. Punishment involves a parent overreacting and going overboard with a consequence. When a child asks why they can't do something, the parent usually responds with, "Because I said so." Punishment does not teach a child new skills or the ability to make decisions on their own. It either crushes the spirit or causes more rebellion. Punishment might include extreme measures like a teen getting grounded indefinitely, a parent spanking when angry or throwing away toys because he didn't clean his room. Punishments are done to inappropriately control the child.

Disciplining is for the purpose of teaching a child good character and in a way that is calm, loving, firm, and respectful. Discipline teaches a child how to learn from his mistakes and learn new skills, such as how to manage his behaviors, solve problems, and deal with his feelings. It includes things such as time out, privilege withdrawal, and sometimes spanking. The child is given consequences that make sense and are time sensitive. An example for a younger child: "You need to sit in time out for two minutes." Discipline also involves using praise or reward systems. Disciplining your child versus punishing your child will foster the warm, positive relationship with your child that you seek.

> **PARENTING TIP:**
> Nurture if the problematic behavior is caused by something you know your child didn't know how to handle; discipline if you know your child knew the standard and is willfully breaking it.

GETTING CONNECTED

When you parent with warmth, your child will feel connected to you and want to obey you out of respect and wish to please you. For this to happen, you must give your child love and affection and make them feel important and significant to you. Remember you were their age once, so don't minimize their feelings.

STEP 1: Take five
If you want a calm child, you first have to become calm and patient. As you begin to feel your anger rising, take a deep breath and count to five before blowing up, screaming, arguing, criticizing, or conveniently doing the task for the child. If not, chaos will ensue.

This may be hard at first, but it's important to understand that you have been part of the problem and that it's now time to take responsibility for your role for any nagging, arguing or anger outbursts from your child. When that happens, you will begin to show more restraint and patience with your child rather than just flying off the handle or making matters worse.

Don't expect to become calm overnight. At this point, your goal is to try not cave in and to extend the amount of time that you are calm and in control of your emotions. When you do this, you've had a successful exchange and are improving!

In this way, you will build your relationship through successful exchanges and "battles won." Think of it as an act of courage that will build your character and your child's. *You and your child win when you stay calm. You and your child lose when you lose it.*

> **PARENTING TIP:**
> Speak softly when your child defies or disrespects you to calm both of you down. This method can also help you to manage the situation. Walk away if you can't handle your emotions.

STEP 2: Give your child one-on-one time
Take at least 20 minutes a day for one-on-one time with your child. Listen to him, show genuine interest, and try to become aware of his feelings. Maybe everything is fine and this is just a special time between you and him. Or perhaps he is having a problem and feels lonely, depressed, frightened, angry, sad, or frustrated and needs your pursuit. Rather than have him retreat to his room and avoid life, you, the parent, can ask, "What is the reason for your feelings?" "Are you having problems with family, friends, school, or your health?"

Try to identify the problem. Perhaps he's being bullied or worried about a test or feeling unpopular. Or perhaps he is spending too much time alone because both of you are working parents or you are a single parent, and he has too many responsibilities for a child his age. If he's upset about something, try to brainstorm solutions with him. This will help ground him and connect to you.

Reassure him that things will get better. Give him advice on how to fix it or create a strategy for solving the problem, even if that means you have to advocate for him. Continue to follow up until the problem is resolved.

Also assure him that things will get better in the house. Tell him, "You *will* be peaceful. We are *all* going to be more peaceful." Repeat this statement as many times as necessary. Believe it. Then, your child will.

When you get better at listening and discerning how your child feels, your parent/child relationship will improve drastically. I have had many parents tell me that when they began to show more patience and interest in their child and became more aware of their own personal emotional status, their child became significantly happier and more cooperative.

> **PARENTING TIP:**
> Try to slow and calm things down in the home by using a soft voice with a low intensity.

STEP 3: Communicate with your child

Focus on communicating more with your children. Ask specific questions about their schooling, their classes, their jobs, their friends. Call their friends by name. If you don't know them, inquire about them.

STEP 4: Apply as many "emotional connectors" as possible

INDIVIDUAL AND FAMILY FUN TIME

Family Fun Time is a great way for the family to connect and build unity as everyone enjoys each other. It will also help your child feel less depressed or lonely, especially a teenager. And when you consistently make the time for your child, especially if he is currently acting out, perhaps this will give him the attention he may be crying out for.

You should schedule fun time both with your child one-on-one and as a family.

There are many activities you can do alone with your child or all together:

- Play board games
- Cook or bake something special

- Go to a park and play an outdoor activity
- Go to the movies or watch a movie at home and pop some popcorn
- Do a dance-off or sing karaoke
- Play video games
- Go to a skating rink, bowling alley, or video games arcade
- Go on a picnic
- Throw a football, shoot some hoops, paint some fingernails, read a book, etc.

Family Dinners

It's important for you to all eat together as a family four-five times per week if possible (minimum three times weekly). No TV or other electronics. Everyone shares in preparing dinner and in the clean-up. Dinner is slow and leisurely and focuses on questions to the children about their day. For example: "How was math today?" "Who did you play with on the playground today?" "Who did you 'hang out' with today at lunch and how has he been doing?"

Discuss specific subjects and the classes you suspect your child to have homework in. Inquire about upcoming tests and the studying plan. Maybe you will want to "go around the table" and get an expression of "the highlight of the day" and ask if there were any "low points." Just the fact that your family is undivided and connected during this time is powerful. Schedule this time together weekly.

Notes to Child

Writing notes to your child can help you express feelings that may be difficult for you to show but that will greatly improve your parent/child connection. Writing something like, "You know, son, I may not have all the answers at this moment for your behavior, but I'm working on it" will help cement your relationship with your child.

Forgive your child

It's important to not hold grudges for your child's rebellious and disrespectful behaviors. Forgive your child as quickly as possible, *no matter what the infraction.* Follow up with your child later that same day to reinforce your commitment to his good character and how much you love him. He needs to know you will not stop trying to teach him good lessons in life. Compliment him for something he did right.

Creating new standards for your relationship for now and the future is a powerful activity that can also help break up any long-standing anger and resentment. Tomorrow's a new day; make it a fresh start.

Apologize

Ask your child for forgiveness if you have been too harsh, punitive, or permissive. Sincerely promise to try to lead differently, and discuss with your child or teen how you plan to do this. This may be difficult to do, but it shows your child that you are sensitive to having hurt him and wish to make amends. In so doing, you will help your child to develop a healthy sense of guilt and remorse when he does something wrong, and in time, he will apologize spontaneously, indicating that your teaching principles are working.

Try the following when you've made a mistake:

- Acknowledge how you were wrong for what you did.
- Sincerely apologize and try hard to not offend again.

STEP 5: Pick your battles

Don't micromanage your child for every little thing. If not going to bed at a reasonable time has been a source of arguments for a long time, avoid this well-known battle for now. When you begin to execute some of the strategies we've been talking about, your child may want to change this behavior on his own.

Parenting as a Team

Weekly Parent Business Meetings

First set the kids up doing something productive and then take some time for yourselves to discuss important issues, such as planning a budget or family issues. Discuss the topic of discipline for the kids or whatever problems the family may have that needs addressing such as finances, who will transport kids to "extracurriculars," which nights can be family dinner nights, etc. Schedule 1-2 meetings weekly for 45 minutes or so. Sunday afternoons may be a good time for parents to meet. If the parents are happy, everyone is happy!

Guiding Child through School

One parent needs to volunteer to be the child's learning guide who will superintend, oversee, and spearhead his scholastic efforts. The other parent should be supportive. You are responsible for making sure that your child is fitting in to the school he attends, understanding, learning the material, and making at least the minimum grade you allow in each class.

Creating Structure

The Weekend Organizer

You should plan the family's events for the upcoming weekend and put it onto the Weekend Organizer so that the whole family can see it. Putting it on the refrigerator is a good idea. Include also any consistent activities, such as attending church as well as when you and your spouse will have your Weekly Parent Business Meeting.

In my house, we post a Weekend Organizer by Tuesday or Wednesday. We have found that this helps balance the pace of our social activities to avoid unnecessary stressing. You can declare the upcoming Friday, Saturday, and Sunday "unplanned" if you choose, and this can help give your family much needed rest, something a lot of busy families are missing.

If you happen to get a last minute invitation to an event, stop and think, consult with your spouse, and refer to your Weekend Organizer before making a decision. This process can help you to maintain family peace.

Weekend Organizer Sample

Friday, _____ (date)

- Family Movie Night

Saturday, _____ (date)

- Grandpa's Birthday Party
  2:00 p.m.- 4:00 p.m.

Sunday, _____ (date)

- Church - leave by 10 a.m.
    - 8:30 Breakfast
    - 9:00 Get dressed & ready
    - 9:55 Kids ready and wait by door
- Plan upcoming week's menu
- Start next Weekend Organizer

Leave the Home Calmly and Orderly

When you are planning to leave your home, let your child know at minimum 45-60 minutes in advance the time you plan to leave. Also, tell him he needs to be in the car or sitting by the door fully ready five minutes prior. He can follow your instructions while you finish what you are doing in the house. Then you join the family at the scheduled time to leave. Leading in this fashion can be a big help organizationally, give the family a structure to count on, and give you time to think twice about making sure you have all you need for your trip.

Walk Together as a Family

Walk together as a family unit or side by side, whether you are getting out of your car, leaving a place of business, or strolling through the mall.

- For a younger child, play "follow the leader," have him hold your hand, or have him walk alongside you. These approaches work really well for children who are overly active and impulsive and can even prevent a child from running out in front of a car.

- For a teenager, this concept of walking together will promote family cohesion.

Chapter Three

Transforming the Attitudes

Parents need to be in tune to what their child needs spiritually, emotionally, academically, and socially.

You will transform your parent/child relationship by implementing the very powerful combination of parenting principles below:

Have Faith

Believe right now that you will defeat the defiant attitude and gain a healthy control of your parent/child relationship. It must be earned with a warm but firm attitude and with the knowledge and application of certain parenting skills. A strong-willed child will not give you the control easily.

Stay Focused

Focus your awareness on being more patient and remaining calm at all times. This will show your child respect and he will not only respect you back but also obey and follow your leadership.

Set a Vision

Set a vision for your family relationships. Set some expectations. Discuss your heart's desire for a peaceful home. Set your intentions to better manage your own anger and anxiety. Vow to nurture your child by spending more quality time together.

Take a Discipline Vacation

Cease disciplining your child until you are ready to present him with *The Family Check System (FCS)* and instead educate your family on your new expectations. This "vacation" only applies temporarily, while you are creating the FCS, and is necessary so that you can distance yourself from the drama and effectively regroup. These strategies play a major role in your transformation from chaos to peace!

In place of discipline, focus on being calm and patient, educating, setting new expectations, learning new skills, and taking new steps towards peaceful living. Make the conscious decision to take a break from the heavy, tense, or prolonged punishments and arguments. Do not be concerned with character shaping during this transformational phase of the *FC2P Program*. Focus on practicing the approaches in this chapter until you achieve an acceptable level of peaceful relations in your family. You will be ready to shape and mold your child's character once you have gained his respect as evidenced by his increased cooperation level.

Family Meeting Types

Family meetings allow discussion of the problems the child and family have been encountering, along with what to do to change the situation. You can use the family meeting at different times, depending on need.

The Anytime Family Meeting

It's a good idea for the whole family to get together *anytime* you believe there is a need. Typically the weekend is a good time to discuss concerns, plans, behavior issues, and complaints. This opens up parent/child communication and also gives your child empowerment in the whole *FC2P Program* to help create mutual respect between parent and child. Allow up to 15 minutes for communicating any new information as well as changes to any of the three plans: *Routine*, *Discipline*, and *Reward*.

The Lemonade Meeting

When things get too heated or intense or when any urgent matter pops up, call a 45 minute "Lemonade Meeting." This needs to be a private meeting between you and the defiant child. Set up the other children with an activity.

Have some lemonade around the table to diffuse the issues. Talk it out, listen, take notes. You may even use a journal for the purpose of guiding the meeting.

Your family has gotten too flustered and you need to help them with expressing themselves and being heard. Your role is to listen and allow your children to be heard. You will be the secretary and will take notes of what is said so that in time the problems will be solved or at least addressed.

During this meeting, if you want the lying or bullying behaviors to stop, say so. If you want hitting to stop, say so. If you want to go to your place of worship more, say so. If you are sick and tired of the 3-D's (disobedience, disrespect, and defiance), say so! This meeting will be successful when you maintain control by communicating expectations but more importantly if your child feels heard. So go for it!

THE DAILY AFTER-SCHOOL HOMEWORK MEETING

It's important to stay on top of what goes on at school. Allow 10-15 minutes for the purpose of helping your child with developing organizational skills, creating a study plan, and to discuss homework, field trips, parent need for involvement in school activities, etc. This will enable you to make sure your child stays on track and allow you to have time to prepare for what you need to do to insure your child's school success.

THE FCS IMPLEMENTATION MEETING

Allow 45-60 minutes for the sole purpose of presenting *The Family Check System* to your child. Take on the patience of a teacher and educate your child on your new expectations you have for your family.

FAMILY MEETING RULES

- The family will talk with respect for the others which means no name calling, blaming, and shaming.
- An acceptable tone of voice is required.

- If you can't control your emotions, walk away, but before you do, communicate when you will reconvene. If your child follows you, try to not lose your temper.

USE A PERSONAL GROWTH NOTEBOOK

Make a notebook for your child and put his name on it for use now and in the future. Use this tool when you are having difficulty teaching your child chores like cleaning the kitchen or doing the laundry. The focus should be on the child doing a chore to a reasonable standard based on him doing his best. For example, for the chore "Clean the kitchen," you should list in your Personal Growth notebook:

1. All table tops wiped down.
2. Sink emptied.
3. Floors swept.

Spending extra time to have a family meeting and write out the steps to a particular chore that your child is not doing to your satisfaction can be transformational. Once your child understands your expectation and initials the steps in his Personal Growth Notebook, you can, with a clear conscience, set a standard and a consequence.

The Personal Growth Notebook can also be used for a child who has emotional issues caused by certain triggers like medicine taking and hormonal changes. For example, your child may throw a temper tantrum daily when it comes to medicine taking. You as the parent, knowing that the medicine is necessary, need to take the extra time to nurture your child and create a plan that is reasonable such as:

1. Mom will have a glass of chocolate milk ready for you when you awaken.
2. You will take your medicine without fussing.
3. If you resist, there will be a consequence.

This tool is versatile and can help with the teaching of chores, good character, and any expectations you have to help your child cope better with life situations and not use situations as excuses for bad behavior. Write out realistic steps, hold them accountable, and watch your child grow!

Chapter Four

IMPROVING PARENTING SKILLS

*Parents need wisdom in decision making,
emotional strength to lead appropriately,
and discernment to discover truth.*

Journaling

To understand what triggers your child's defiance or disruptive behavior, journal each episode. Walk around your home with a pen and a notebook like a scientist gathering information and let your child know what you are doing and why. "I am writing down what is going on now so I can figure out why this is happening." This will build trust and respect.

The "Direct Assertively" Skill

To help you overcome the traps of arguing, yelling, nagging, avoiding confrontation, and other behaviors that diminish or destroy parent/child relationships, you need to learn how to parent authoritatively to improve parent/child communications. This method may go against your natural tendencies but is necessary as you change chaos to peace. Work hard at mastering the following steps. They will help you to begin restoring and improving your relationship with your child. Implement the "Direct Assertively" skill until your child obeys and respects you more often. This skill is very important!

STEP 1: Get the attention of your child, from the same room, while you become quiet and still.

- Ask child to stop what they are doing, if applicable.

STEP 2: Make eye contact.

- Insist on eye contact, if you have to, *without* inflaming your child.
- Get down on bended knee to talk with a smaller child.

STEP 3: Clearly communicate your instructions.

- "I need" statements can work well. "I need for you to pick up your clothes and put them in the hamper."
- If needed, use a non-verbal cue such as "a look" to make it clear that you are going to see to it that he obeys. Be persistent with

your purposeful gaze. Kids need to know that you are serious about them following through with your expectations.

You may also want to use verbal cues like: "*Did you hear what I asked you to do?*" (Expect compliance); "*Repeat back to me what I asked you to do so I know that you heard me.*" (Expect cooperation).

- If a child is really stubborn, deliver instructions without child's eye contact.
  - ⇒ If this is the case, obtaining eye contact will be something you and your child will need to work on. Very important for quality communications.

STEP 4: Be polite and say "thank you" once you know your instructions have been received. A "yes" or "yes, ma'am" from your child is a good indicator.

STEP 5: Give your child up to five minutes to begin carrying out your instructions.

THE "DEAL WITH DEFIANCE" SKILL

The "Deal with Defiance" skill, like the Discipline Vacation strategy, will be used only in the first part of the *FC2P Program*. Once you create and implement *The Family Check System*, you will learn new skills in Chapter 7, like the Warning, Strike 1, Strike 2, or Strike 3 method that will replace them.

Use the following steps to improve parental authority and parent/child empathy if your child has ignored your first attempt to "Direct Assertively":

STEP 1: Repeat the "Direct Assertively" steps.

This time raise the volume and intensity of your voice just a bit so your child knows that you are serious about them doing what you ask. Be firmer this time, without yelling and condescending. If the child still does not comply with your requests this second time, follow through with Steps 2 and 3 below.

STEP 2: Use an "I feel" statement which will help in developing empathy, a key to satisfying relationships.

Examples include:

- "I really don't appreciate you challenging my authority. At the moment, I feel very frustrated with you!"

- "It makes me feel disappointed that you are choosing to behave so stubbornly."

> **Parenting Tip:**
> Deliver "I feel" statements with sincerity, not anger.

STEP 3: Walk away from the child.
Do whatever needs to be done, even if you have to do what you asked your child to do. This is not enabling your child at this early stage of the program but preparing the way for effective discipline. Think of it as child management.

Commit to Keeping Your Cool

Focus on practicing and mastering the skills of "Direct Assertively" and "Deal with Defiance," while keeping your cool. You will learn new effective disciplinary approaches later that will help you to shape and mold the character of your child. As for now, you will need to focus on disconnecting from your old ways of doing things to set the stage for new disciplinary methods and structure. Work on interacting appropriately and lovingly with your child. This will go a long way toward improving your parent/child relationship!

Commit to Toughening Up Emotionally

Focus on being less reactive and less pushy. When you do not fire back and don't force things, you are improving your emotional strength and self-control which are required to parent effectively.

Do this by choosing just the right time to overcome your child's opposition, like when he is calmer, and have patience in doing so. In a sense, you are developing emotional toughness—being able to, at times, deal with "a little more of your child's attitude" in a more productive way. Sometimes we need to be able to tolerate a little of our teenager's angst and follow up with them later. Occasionally accepting some of your child's emotionality helps them to grow as an individual and goes with the territory of parenthood.

At other times you will want to become still when your child is disobedient, make eye contact (but not glares), cast your eyes away, or simply walk away. Become stronger at ignoring nagging and hateful behaviors and learn to tolerate your child when he ignores you. These can be the approaches that help give you the edge in overcoming your child's defiance!

PART 2

Creating and Implementing The Family Check System

Chapter Five

LEADING AND GUIDING WITH PURPOSE

The best teacher in the world for your child is <u>you.</u>

The *Family Check System*, which consists of the *Routine, Discipline,* and *Reward Plans,* will help you to lead and guide your child better with the purpose of strengthening his character. You will create each type of plan for each child, have a family meeting to discuss it, and then start implementing it.

The function of *The Family Check System* is to help you set up a plan of action that gives your child routines to follow which provide structure, an opportunity for reward when he makes good choices, and consequences for poor choices. In the next chapters, you will learn how to create each of the plans of *The Family Check System,* depending on the age and developmental level of your child.

For any of you who have ever watched a cooking show and observed how one of the contestants prepares, cooks, and serves the judges for a ruling as to whether or not their dish tastes good, you have observed "these steps." Child training is much the same.

Just as cooks clean their surfaces and disinfect the cooking areas in order to prepare the dish, parents plan for the good behavior of their children by planning routines, standards, consequences, and rewards to attain family peace. Just as the cook gets out the ingredients, pre-heats the skillet, adds the ingredients, and stirs, the parent can use the three plans (*Routine, Discipline,* and *Reward*) in an effort to attain peace, cooperation, mutual trust, and respect. Just as the cook carefully watches over the dish to assure thorough cooking and that they do not burn the meal, the effective parent will do the same, carefully watching over the children and family to assure no one becomes inflamed. And just as the cook will remove the dish at the right time for everyone's eating pleasures and serve, the effective parent will practice their parenting until they know just when, what, and how to apply their plans and do so consistently until peace has been achieved. Peace and happiness has happened for many and it can happen for you.

Basic Guidelines

Plan Well

Take your time in planning your *Family Check System* so it meets the needs of your particular child.

Sticktuit

Determine to implement the *The Family Check System* to the end as its success is based on your willingness to follow through consistently for at least a month without exception and with all three parts—*Routine Plan, Discipline Plan, and Reward Plan*. At this time you should begin to see a major shift in the family dynamics. When you enact routines with a good balance of rules, consequences, and rewards, your child will learn new skills and approaches and do what you ask him to do without you pushing or forcing. The full desired result typically takes hold within a few months.

> **Parenting Tip:**
> When it is made crystal clear *who* the disciplinarian will be, the child gains clarity and behaviors improve, provided there is a "well thought out" behavior plan and a parent who is committed to following through with it.

Q&A

How should I approach my child about *The Family Check System*?

- To get your child on board, tell them that you want to give *The Family Check System* a try. This is a respectful, non-threatening approach. Begin your conversation by stating the goal is to help everyone be more accountable for their actions. Explain briefly what *The Family Check System* is and let your child know you are in the process of creating one for him. Tell your child that you will keep him posted as to when it is finished so that you and he can meet and discuss how *The Family Check System* is designed to help your family.

How do I present multiple *Family Check Systems* to my kids?

- Try to have your FCS Implementation Meeting with the whole family. It may be wise to have individual FCS Implementation Meetings to assure that you are communicating well with each child. Individualized attention can foster a deeper understanding from your child.

How do I lead the FCS Implementation Meeting?

- Review the *Routine Plan* until you are sure your child understands what is expected.

- Tell the three- to six-year-olds that you need them to follow their *Routine Plan* as you have directed them.

- Convey clear instructions on your *standards*, *methods* for correcting misbehavior, and *consequences* for not doing what is asked of them.

- State that you have some responsibilities as do they and that creating peace will be a "team effort." Communicate some of your responsibilities like superintending the *Routine Plan*, following through with consequences as well as with rewards.

- Review your child's *Reward Plan* with them. The sign of a strong *Reward Plan is* when your child shows approval; this will be validation that you have prepared a motivating plan.

- Once you have explained to your child his *Family Check System*, have him initial all three plans along with you indicating an agreement. This will show his acknowledgment of what you are implementing and allow for accountability.

- Anytime there is a change in *The Family Check System* like an alteration in the *Routine, Discipline,* or *Reward Plans*, make sure you communicate this to your family. Effective and consistent communication between you and your child is a key to your success. Your leadership and guidance and your consistent stand for your rules will forge a peaceful and loving environment for you and your family.

- Inform your child as to when you want to start *The Family Check System*. You can start today or pick a day very soon.

How much time should I allow for presenting *The Family Check System* to my child?
Allow 45-60 minutes to explain all three plans of *The Family Check System* to your child and to insure their understanding.

What if my child is disagreeable and resisting *The Family Check System* when I present it?
If your child has a bad attitude, encourage him without losing patience and becoming disrespectful. If necessary, have a second *FCS* Implementation Meeting within 24 hours to cement your intentions on the new way you plan on leading. Persist with your plan and don't give up as your child will accept *The Family Check System* with your persistence and emotional strength.

> **PARENTING TIP:**
> Do not discipline while you are creating the three plans. Instead take advantage of teachable moments by educating your child on the changes you intend on making. For example, "Back talking will not be tolerated; I'm working on a plan for that." Continue improving your relationship with your child by using the "Direct Assertively" and "Deal with Defiance" skills and by having quality time with them.

Do I have to implement all three plans?
The *Routine* and *Discipline Plans* are a necessity. The *Reward Plan* can be optional if for some reason your child rejects it. It is very unlikely your child will reject your reward for respectful behavior, if it is something that the child likes very much like a monetary commission, use of electronics, or hanging out with friends.

> **PARENTING TIP:**
> When introducing the routines your child is to follow, anticipate that he may test you and stand firm! Do not fall into the trap of arguing when your child disrespects, nags, or begs. Set a limit while keeping cool and move on to the next thing on the agenda.

What do we do if we begin *The Family Check System* prematurely and find ourselves overwhelmed and frequently arguing?
Should this happen, use it as a time to model proper behavior to your children and apologize for your overreaction. Dust yourself off and hopefully you'll be able to offer and receive hugs and kisses as symbols of forgiveness. Then go back to your planning, complete it, and implement it properly.

Chapter Six

Routine Planning

*Being a parent involves teaching a child self-control,
respect for authority, and consideration for others and their rules.*

One of the biggest reasons for chaos in the family is confusion and instability from lack of structure or order. It's imperative to create structure if you want peace in your home. The way to do this is through predictable routines for tasks, chores, or duties from getting ready to go to school in the morning to preparing for bedtime. In this chapter, you will learn how to create a family roadmap of daily and weekly routines so your children know what is expected of them and what comes next.

Routine Plans

- School

- Holiday

- Summer

Routine Plan Components

- AM and PM routines.

- Pictured routine for the child who has not yet learned to read. Use drawings, actual photos of child doing the particular tasks, or any other picture that clearly represents the task to the child. The very first *Routine Plan* our family used was the Pictured Routine for our children who at the time were between the ages of three to six. This tool gave our family much needed structure, and our children were very willing to participate.

- This same level of cooperation carried over as the children got older, learned how to read, and began to learn what a commission was.

- Written routine for the older child or teenager.

> **PARENTING TIP:**
> It is important for you to have a routine also. Start your routine by getting out of bed at least 15 minutes before your child, so that you are ready to greet him peacefully and supervise his routine. Recall the Eversley family successfully turned their family from one of chaos to peace. The mom stated that awakening and getting up before the children helped significantly in terms of her presence and authority.

Checkpoints

The checkpoint is what you will use throughout the day to check that your child has followed the AM/PM routines. You will "superintend" and check at least two times, three if the child misbehaves in more than one location (for example, at home with parents *and* at school with teachers.) *The Family Check System* is aimed at buttressing your authority as a parent, hence the "checks" and "checkpoints." When the check is earned, you will direct your child to his *Reward Plan* where he will mark his check.

Checkpoint Times

Consider where you want the checkpoints. Here are some possibilities:

- **Home:** You deliver checks after the AM and PM routines are complete.
- **School:** You deliver checks for performance and behavior once school is complete.
- **Special Routines:** You deliver checks for after school activities like dance, sports, cheerleading, music, etc. if applicable.
- **Weekend Routines:** You deliver checks for weekend routines

such as chores and church, depending on how much structure is needed by the child on weekends.

- **Other:** You deliver checks for behavior in other environments, like Grandma's house where your child spends the morning while you work.

> **PARENTING TIP:**
> Some parents make their own variation of the checkpoint process and may carry a notebook to keep up with the discipline or rewards of the day. Whatever approach you use for your checkpoints, the key is to keep consistency in communication and in following through with your expectations for him.

CHECKPOINT PROCESS

For the first two weeks of implementation, you will remind your child at the end of each routine, if for some reason they forget, it is time for them to ask for their check. After *The Family Check System* has been in effect for two weeks or so, it is the child's responsibility to ask for a check. Little kids especially love this part of the program as it makes them feel like a big boy. Show some excitement as you praise your child for behaving so appropriately and pressing onward toward his reward. Here's an example:

Child: "May I have my check?"

Parent: "What have you done?" "What did you do?"

Child: "I cleaned up my room." "I did not argue with you when you told me I can't have candy before dinner." "I said, 'Yes, sir' when you called my name."

Parent: Say excitedly, "Go put a check on your *Reward Plan*."

Superintend and follow through. When the checkpoint process is enforced consistently, this will help to strengthen your relationship with your child.

> **PARENTING TIP:**
> By overseeing and managing your child's routines consistently, you are committing to assisting your child with an overall feeling of security and well-being while at the same time maintaining a spirit of togetherness and teamwork for the family.

ROUTINE PLAN TIPS

- Approximately two weeks before the start of a new season and a new routine, begin your routine planning. Remember to have a family meeting before the start date of your new routine. Two weeks should give you and your family enough time to begin effectively transitioning into the new routine.

- Be clear in devising your plans. Write them out neatly and clearly and make certain that your child can read it.

- Be specific in listing all the tasks you want your child to be responsible for and the times you want them done.

- Make your routine reasonable and peaceful by allowing enough time for each task or set of tasks to be easily done.

- Base your routine plans on your child's developmental level:
  ⇒ Devise a pictured routine for the child who has not yet learned to read.
  ⇒ Devise a written routine for the older child or teenager.

- Choose by time of year:
  - ⇒ School Routine
  - ⇒ Summer Routine
  - ⇒ Holiday Routine
- Make your routine easy by rounding off the times to five-minute increments in which you want the task to be done. (6:00, 6:05, 6:10.) Also for the sake of flow, you can merge multiple tasks together. ("Get out of bed, get dressed, and have breakfast by 7:00.")
- Encourage your child to relax but also to keep moving through the routine. No rushing.
- Sunday evenings are the most important time for the school routine in terms of getting off to a strong start on the week.
- Always include checkpoints in your routine to keep your child on track.
- Once *FCS* is complete, have your child place one in his bedroom or bathroom and you keep one in the kitchen area along with *Discipline* and *Reward Plans*.
- In addition to planning routines, also use the Weekend Organizer to help manage upcoming events that change from week to week.
- On Friday nights and Saturday mornings, you may allow your child to relax a bit by not having to meet checkpoints. If so, you will want to put an "X" on the corresponding boxes on the *Reward Plan* indicating these times are not available for checks.
- In the event that your child is not cooperating with his AM/PM routine and has earned a Warning or Strike, instruct him to write it on the dry erase board. Then, have him go back and finish his routine if you have time.

- The only way your child does not get the check is if he does not finish the routine on time. It is possible for your child to get a Warning and even a Strike and finish his routine on time and earn his check.

- Make sure that the number of tasks and the intensity of each are realistic for your child. You can always eliminate a task from the routine if in retrospect you figure you have expected too much. Remember, you can always start a routine 15 minutes earlier to help your child be more successful.

> **PARENTING TIP:**
> *The Routine Plan* is one plan to which you may want to make periodic adjustments. As circumstances change, you will want to make the effort to review and change the order of things or simply add or delete tasks and activities. Keep it current. This is commonly done before the school year begins or between semesters.

How To Create Your Child's Routine Plan

STEP 1
On a blank computer document or sheet of paper put your child's name at the top and behind it the type of Routine Plan (School, Holiday, Summer). See the samples below.

STEP 2
Beginning with the AM Routine, list out all of the times and tasks that need to be achieved as part of your child's routine. Five minutes before the last task of the AM Routine, schedule a checkpoint.

STEP 3
Begin your PM Routine and create it in the same manner as the AM Routine.

STEP 4
After most or all the major tasks are done, schedule a checkpoint on the PM Routine to keep everything on track and all accountable.

> **Parenting Tip:**
> If your child is working diligently but is unable to complete his work by the agreed upon time frame, acknowledge your child's efforts and grant him more time. If this becomes a pattern, adjust the child's routine to allow extra time.

Sample Routine Plans

Use the following sample *Routine Plans* as your guide:

Summer Routine Sample
Five-year-old Boy

SCHOOL ROUTINE SAMPLE
Ten-year-old Boy

Sunday PM*–Friday AM

AM Routine

6:40	Alarm and get up
By 7:20	Get dressed, wash face, brush hair, and put on shoes
7:30	Breakfast time
By 7:50	Brush teeth, get book bag
7:55	Checkpoint
8:00	Start heading to school

PM Routine

3:20	Empty book bag. Hang it up.
3:30–4:00	Have a snack, start homework

On Tuesdays, get ready for drum lesson
Get your homework, be in the car **by 4:15**

*By 6:00	Take shower, set out clothes, prepare for school and set alarm for next day
	Help set out drinks for dinner
6:15	Family dinner
	Brush and floss teeth
	Free time
By 8:00	Checkpoint
By 8:15	In bedroom
9:00	Lights out and "nighty-nite"

School Routine Sample
Sixteen-year-old Boy and Thirteen-year-old Girl

Sunday PM*–Friday AM Routine

AM Routine

6:30	Victor—Alarm, up, shower/deodorant/dress
7:00	Leslie—Alarm, up, dressed
7:20-7:40	Family Breakfast
7:40-8:00	Make beds, tidy room, clean vanity, pick up dirties, brush teeth, ready for the day
8:00	Checkpoint—Routine done!
8:05	Victor—Bus stop; Leslie—Walk to school

PM Routine

3:00	Arrive home, get a snack, and have free time
4:00	Homework
5:30	Dinner
*By 6:00	Finish homework or evening activities
	Monday 6:00–7:00 Leslie—Cheer
	6:30–7:30 Victor—Band
	Wednesday 6:00–7:00 Leslie—Cheer
	7:00–7:30 Victor—Piano
8:00	Leslie—Shower
	Both—Set out clothes, set alarms, brush and floss teeth
8:30	Checkpoint
	Evening routine done, electronic devices on cabinet
By 8:35	Bedroom time, quiet reading
9:15	Victor—Lights out
9:30	Leslie—Lights out

PARENTING TIP:

Always have a good plan for your child after school, especially if he gets home before you do. Give him realistic instructions he can follow and include a phone contact time where you can touch base. Expecting him to complete all of his homework immediately after he gets home may be unrealistic and frustrating for all. It may be better to instruct him to have a snack and complete a chore or have free time. Let your child know that when you get home, he will need to be settled down and ready to do his homework. This will teach him responsibility.

Chapter Seven

Discipline Planning

Although your child may not tell you directly, they yearn for you to manage their disruptive behaviors and help them resolve any problems.

In this chapter, you will learn methods, principles, and guidelines of discipline for your child. The backbone of *The Family Check System*—the *Discipline Plan*—consists of your standards and expectations for your child's behavior and consequences if the family standards or rules are broken. When combined, they can create character in your child, from obeying and respecting authority to truth telling to being kind to others.

> **PARENTING TIP:**
> Persist in doing whatever it takes, regardless of the time, to stop the defiance and then maintain the peace once it is achieved.

COMMON PARENTING PITFALLS TO AVOID

- Lack of patience with your child
- Reactive punishing "from the hip" whereby you constantly create new consequences
- Feeling too frustrated to control anger
- Failing to apologize
- Failing to follow through with the agreed-upon responsibilities of *The Family Check System*.

PARENTING TIP:
Before disciplining your child, consider what caused the behavior:

- Could it be from fatigue?
- Has something unexpected happened (the big game got cancelled)?
- Does Dad now have to work longer hours?
- Did the child stay up too late last night?
- Is the child sick?
- Was the routine altered unexpectedly?
- Did you the parent disrupt things? (By losing your temper or enforcing the rules of the house inconsistently?)
- Was he stressed by too many activities and needed more down time?

In any of these situations, you may want to be lenient and compassionate if your child has a minor melt down. After all, maybe he just needs an extra dose of patience and love.

How To Create Your Child's Discipline Plan

The primary components to the *Discipline Plan* are standards and consequences.

STEP 1

Check off standards that need improving from the following (add in your own):

STANDARDS

You expect your child to obey you, to follow your instructions quickly, and to behave appropriately. That means:

- ☐ **Obey Quickly and Respect Parent**

    Note that obedience, respect, and cooperation are already included in each *Discipline Plan* template since they are the most problematic behaviors for parents.

- ☐ **Respect Siblings**

    Be kind and loving towards siblings. No getting in their space, taking things away, bullying, inflaming, arguing, taunting, name calling, being selfish, self-centeredness, etc.

- ☐ **Follow House Rules**
    - Wait your turn to speak; no interrupting.
    - Snacks should be at least 45 minutes before mealtime.
    - No shoes on furniture.
    - Always ask and confirm permission from parents before leaving the house.
    - No leaving a family meeting without asking permission from parents.

- No laziness. Be responsible with work and chores. No shirking responsibilities like not finishing lawn care or doing a good job once trained.
- Be polite by showing good manners at the table and considerate by picking up after self.
- Eating must be limited to kitchen area unless otherwise approved.
- No crude or immodest behaviors.

☐ **Behave Morally and Ethically**
- No illegal behaviors such as substance use. No alcohol, drugs, tobacco; stealing; property damage, etc.
- No sexual activity.
- Be respectful to property (toys, telephones, etc.). No destruction or being too rough.
- No lying to get out of trouble. Tell the whole truth, no omissions, spinning, or part truths.
- Be kind to others: No hitting, kicking, spitting, biting, sitting on, tackling or body-slamming people, play touching, or scaring.

☐ **Behave Appropriately in School**
- Turn in all assignments; no zeros.
- No cheating.
- No disruptive or rebellious behavior in school.
- Take pride in schoolwork and learning.

☐ **Have Wise Electronic Practices**
- No electronics until schoolwork is complete for the day and you have permission.

- Do not exceed maximum time allowed for electronics without permission.
- No use of the internet unless supervised by parent.
- Place electronic device on cabinet before bedtime.
- No contact with people through devices unless parents approve. Kids are responsible for letting parents know of any loopholes.

> **PARENTING TIP:**
> Make certain that the standards you set meet your child's developmental level. For instance, it may not be reasonable to expect a child aged three to seven to comply with the rule of having a high quality of bathing, taking out the trash, or sweeping the floor on his own the first several times. These tasks can take lots of patience and some anger management on your part, and many repetitions by the child before he can be expected to do them with any quality. You may want to use the Personal Growth Notebook in this instance to teach your expectations. This is an excellent teaching tool!

STEP 2

Take the identified standards and place them onto the standards column of the Discipline Plan template found on pages 78 & 79.

You can make copies or create and print out pages based on your child's age. Use the *Discipline Plan* sample on the next page to guide you.

> **PARENTING TIP:**
> Before disciplining your child, consider the following: "Did he know better?" or "Did he actually have no idea as to why he behaved the way he did?" For example, a peer at school convinces your child it's fun to stop up the toilets at school with paper towels, which eventually floods the bathroom. Once a parent has discerned whether or not he knew that what he was doing was wrong or had the social skill to avoid it, a parent can then determine what a proper penalty may be for this. If a child gets duped into this peer situation without knowing how to handle it, it may be appropriate to simply have a discussion with your child and then give a proper warning of an appropriate consequence that will occur if it happens again.

DISCIPLINE PLAN SAMPLE
SEVEN- TO SEVENTEEN-YEAR OLD

STANDARDS	METHOD / CONSEQUENCE
Obey Mom and Dad quickly and be respectful	**Direct child assertively:** "Give yourself a Warning." (put W on board)
No ignoring directions	"Strike 1" (put X on board)
No back talking, talking under breath	"Strike 2" (put another X on board)
Accept "No" for an answer	"Strike 3" = Loss of all electronics for the remainder of today and tomorrow. (video games, TV, phone, tablet)
Eating must be limited to kitchen area unless otherwise approved	Warning, Strike 1, Strike 2, or Strike 3
Tell the truth (no lying)	Automatic Deterrent
No contact with people through electronic devices unless parents approve. Kids are responsible for letting parents know of any loopholes.	Automatic Deterrent
Pick up after yourself— dirty dishes	Extra chore

Child's Name _____ Date _____

Parent's Name _____ Date _____

Parent's Name _____ Date _____

DISCIPLINE PLAN TEMPLATE
Three- to Six-Year-Olds

_____ 's Discipline Plan

STANDARDS	METHOD / CONSEQUENCE
Obey Mom and Dad quickly and be respectful No ignoring directions No back talking, talking under breath Accept "No" for an answer	**Tell child assertively:** "You now have a Warning." "1" "2" "3" = _____ (Deterrent) *If child corrects before "3," restart Warning, 1, 2, or 3 sequence after 20 minutes.
• •	• •

Child's Name _____ Date _____

Parent's Name _____ Date _____

Parent's Name _____ Date _____

DISCIPLINE PLAN TEMPLATE
SEVEN- TO SEVENTEEN-YEAR-OLDS

_____'s Discipline Plan

STANDARDS	METHOD / CONSEQUENCE
Obey Mom and Dad quickly and be respectful	**Direct child assertively:** "Give yourself a Warning." (put W on board)
No ignoring directions	"Strike 1" (put X on board)
No back talking, talking under breath	"Strike 2" (put another X on board)
Accept "No" for an answer	"Strike 3" = _____ _____ (Deterrent) *Each day is a new beginning with a clean board.
• •	• •

Child's Name _____ Date _____

Parent's Name _____ Date _____

Parent's Name _____ Date _____

Discerning Mild, Moderate, and Severe Behaviors

Think of behavior as having three categories: mild, moderate, and severe. The mild behaviors carry a milder consequence such as an additional chore, educational activity, or a small monetary fine. The categories of moderate and severe include the disobedience, disrespect, and defiance of authority and/or high risk behaviors, which require a deterrent. Step three describes how you can create this special consequence known as the deterrent and apply it effectively to defeat the defiant attitude in your home.

STEP 3

Choose a deterrent that will go on the consequence column of the *Discipline Plan* template.

Deterrents

A deterrent is a consequence you will give for moderate and severe disobedient or disrespectful behavior. Its purpose is to make your child think twice before repeating the misbehavior. If your ten-year old has ignored and defied your instruction four times in a day after demonstrating knowledge of your standards, and as a result loses her electronic privileges for the rest of today and tomorrow, he will likely think twice before challenging your authority again.

Considerations When Choosing a Deterrent

Your deterrent needs to be reasonable. If it isn't, it not only won't work but will exacerbate the misbehavior. As an example, the school calls that your teen has been sassing a teacher. As a deterrent, you take away his prized cell phone for a week, which is devastating for any teen today. He is infuriated and back talks to you as well as having disrespected his teacher. You tack on another week and before you know it, he has lost many weeks and the family is becoming more distressed. Your son now feels helpless and even hopeless and his behavior at school and at home has spiraled to an ugly level. Anything you try to discipline him with has lost its effectiveness. Clearly the punishment was too harsh and backfired and was likely delivered by the parent when incensed, not calm.

The parent needed to come up with a more just deterrent, one that would discourage the child from choosing the defiant behavior again, but not inflame him or make him feel hopeless as in the above cell phone example. For instance, the parent could have taken away his cell phone for just that night. This deterrent would neither be harsh nor paralyzing.

> **PARENTING TIP:**
> The "loss of all electronics, including all devices, games, computers, and TV for the rest of today and tomorrow" is an especially effective consequence for many seven- to seventeen-year-olds. There are, of course, other appropriate privilege removal combinations, depending on your child's developmental level and what your child prioritizes the most. Different children will likely require different deterrents. Anything outside the provision of food, clothing, shelter, schooling, and medical care should be considered. For starters, I suggest the duration of the privilege removal to be "the rest of today and tomorrow," regardless of which privileges you remove.

Deterrent Types

- **Time-out.** This is a good strategy for children aged three to seven. A good rule of thumb is to place the child in time-out one minute for every year he is old. For example, three minutes for a three-year-old, five minutes for a five-year-old. If time out is not helpful, consider one of the other deterrent types.

- **Spanking.** One school of thought is that spanking breeds a violent child. This certainly can be the case if the punishment is delivered violently, in an intimidating fashion, or when a parent is angry. On the other hand, if the parent is calm and reasonable and lets the child know ahead of time that spanking will be the consequence for a certain behavior, it can be an effective method for disciplining a child.
- **Privilege Removal.** You as the parent control all privileges and can remove them as a disciplinary measure.

Now put your chosen deterrent in the consequence column on the *Discipline Plan* template by "3" or "Strike 3".

Trading "Deal with Defiance" for the Warning, Strike 1, Strike 2, or Strike 3 Method

As stated earlier, the "Deal with Defiance" skill is only to be used temporarily before implementing *The Family Check System*. Once your *Family Check System* is created and you are ready to implement, you will replace the "Deal with Defiance" skill with what I call the Warning, Strike 1, Strike 2, or Strike 3 method. For three- to six-year-olds, you will simply use Warning, 1, 2, 3.

The Warning, Strike 1, Strike 2, or Strike 3 method revolutionized our ability to discipline in a reasonable and patient way, which yielded positive results in our home. Some parents have asked, "Why so many steps until you punish them?" The reason is for the purpose of helping parents use their patience instead of overreacting. When parents consistently and persistently use the Warning, Strike 1, Strike 2, or Strike 3 method, they show restraint and patience, which are keys to effectively shaping the character of their child.

The following is a typical scenario I will use to illustrate how you can use the Warning, Strike 1, Strike 2, or Strike 3 method. Note that before you enforce a consequence for your child's disobedience, first, get his attention and give him the opportunity to correct his behavior without being disciplined.

Some ways to do this are:

- Do we need to do "Warning and Strikes"?
- Do you need a "Warning"?

These responses alone may be all you need to motivate him to correct. A correction is all you are looking for, even if he grunts or whines, as long as he's moving in the direction you have requested.

If your child resists your directives, the following examples will demonstrate how the Warning, Strike 1, Strike 2, or Strike 3 method can work for you.

Example of One Long and Intense Episode of Defiance

Let's say you direct your child to pick up his socks and put them in the hamper. If he does not acknowledge your request, be sure to get his attention and use the "Direct Assertively" skill. If your child does not comply, then proceed with the following steps:

1. Issue a "Warning" and have him take accountability for his action by writing a "W" on a dry erase board hung at an agreed-upon location. Then persist with directing him to do what you have asked, now with a firmer tone of voice.

2. If the child continues to refuse to pick up his socks after three to five minutes, tell him, "Go give yourself a Strike. Get up, pick up your socks, and bring them to the hamper, now!" Stand firm and in the same room as him so that he knows you are serious. (If you leave the room, your child will likely think you are not as serious about your request or distracted.) Follow up with a non-verbal cue like "a look" to make it clear that you are going to see to it that he obeys. Check back in three to five minutes.

3. Check if your child has followed through. If he has complied, say, "Thank you." If not, issue a "Strike 2." Wait three to five minutes and follow up again.

4. If the child insists on not following your instructions but instead makes a disrespectful remark, deliver "Strike 3" which equals deterrent: time-out, spanking, or privilege removal.

Child's behavior corrects after deterrent is delivered.

Example for Seven- to Seventeen-Year-Olds during Several Episodes of Defiance through the Course of a Day.

First episode of defiance: Child resists your authority by ignoring your instructions to get out of bed.

Parent: Issue a "warning" and have him put it on the dry erase board with a "W."

Child gets out of bed; defiance resolved.

Second episode of defiance: Child resists your authority by choosing to continue playing after you had delivered assertively the instruction of "Come to dinner."

Parent: Issue a verbal Strike 1 and have him put his consequence on the board with an "X."

Child puts Strike on the board, comes to dinner, his behavior corrects.

Third episode of defiance: Child mumbles something under his breath after you have clearly defined this behavior as disrespectful and informed him of what the consequence would be.

Parent: Deliver Strike 2.

Behavior corrects.

Fourth episode of defiance: Child is disobedient or disrespectful toward your authority for a fourth time in the same day.

Parent: Deliver Strike 3 (which is your deterrent).

Child's behavior corrects.

> **PARENTING TIP:**
> Whatever consequence you choose, be clear about what you will do when a particular rule is broken, and always follow through with it.

PRINCIPLES OF THE WARNING, STRIKE 1, STRIKE 2, OR STRIKE 3 METHOD

- Be as clear as possible about when you will deliver a consequence. If you stick to "disobedience" and "disrespect of your authority," this will keep you safe and consistent. Make sure that you discuss your expectations and communicate them clearly.

- After each verbal consequence (Warning, Strike 1, and Strike 2,) have the child show accountability by marking this consequence on the dry erase board for all to see and for all to be responsible for.

- Allow between three to five minutes in between directives for child to obey and be respectful to avoid inflaming your child.

- Remain calm or you could provoke your child. The way you respond to your child gauges how intense the situation with your child will get. If you stay cool and calm, your child will likely have more self-control. The opposite is true, also.

- Use this method consistently and don't be afraid of repeating the Warning, Strike 1, Strike 2, or Strike 3 method with your child if need be. You have as many warnings and strikes as they need.

- Keep up with any disciplinary 'marks' (warning or strikes) that you have delivered for the older children. If you forget the Strike 1 you delivered this morning, you may lose any credibility you have established with your child. Sometimes a parent will not "track" the disciplinary actions he gave and in doing so will appear lenient, even weak, which can be a set up for the rebellious behavior of your child. Strong-willed kids revel in the attention lapses of their parents and can embarrass you if you are not consistent with following through with the tracking of warnings and strikes or following through with a deterrent.

- If your child has a history of slamming doors and hitting walls (without property damage), name calling or using profanity toward you, you will need to put this on the *Discipline Plan* and the suggested consequence for any of these behaviors would be a Warning or Strike for disrespect.

- In extreme circumstances, where your child is violent or if you feel threatened, call the police or 911. Don't live in fear, let someone know. Share the burden.

> **PARENTING TIP:**
> Remember—Warning, Strike 1, and Strike 2 are verbal consequences and should communicate to your child that he has crossed a boundary or limit you have set. If the behavior persists, issue Strike 3 firmly and follow through with the predetermined deterrent. If your child still doesn't follow your request, inform him that you have as many strikes as he needs and are willing to deliver them and then keep track of the consequences.

Automatic Deterrent for Severe Behaviors

Severe behaviors such as lying, hitting others, underage drinking, etc. warrant an Automatic Deterrent due to the risk potential.

Discipline Planning

STEP 4

Finish your *Discipline Plan* by considering any mild behaviors such as laziness with chores or schoolwork.

Also if you choose reward plans that offer commissions, you can charge a fine for behaviors that are crude, impolite, or immodest. Choose an appropriate consequence to go directly across from each standard selected and place it on the consequence column of the *Discipline Plan*.

Consequence Types for Mild Behaviors

- Extra chore
- Extra educational task
- Monetary fine
- Warning, Strike 1, Strike 2, or Strike 3

If you need more examples and suggestions regarding standards and consequence choices, turn to the Appendix (pages 115-118).

> **PARENTING TIP:**
> Once you have completed your *Discipline Plan*, save it along with your *Routine Plan* until you have created the *Reward Plan* and are ready to present all three. (Remember the *Discipline Plan* sample on page 77.)

Discipline Guidelines

- Whatever deterrent you choose, go with it for at least a month upon the presentation of your *Family Check System*. Then make any necessary adjustments with a family meeting.
- It is helpful and clear for a child and parents to create one strong deterrent for all moderate and severe behaviors.

- Have kids initial the *Discipline Plan* for accountability purposes.

- Do not deviate from the *Discipline Plan*. This is a common trap and error for parents. I call this phenomena "reactive discipline." This is when a parent gets frustrated and instead of following the plan, he adds something extra that makes the punishment worse than had been previously agreed on. This action can damage your relationship with your child. He will see this as an abuse of power and may rebel.

- Discipline reasonably, gradually, firmly, and sometimes persistently.

- Remember that the consequence should fit the action of your child. The goal is to teach, not punish or humiliate.

- Before disciplining your child for a broken rule, always discern whether or not your child understands what is expected of him. To do this, ask him to repeat back what you just told him to do. If he doesn't understand, try repeating the instructions in different ways until he demonstrates understanding.

- Make certain that the consequence or penalty is appropriate for the child.

- Address every act of disobedience and rebellious behavior in the same day it occurs if possible.

- To help you deliver the Warning, Strike 1, Strike 2, or Strike 3 method, role play your delivery with your spouse or good friend. Be sure they check you on firmness, tone of voice, body language, and facial expressions. All are very important to effective management of children as you become a stronger disciplinarian.

- Do not make discipline retroactive, in case you find out about a behavior that has been going on for some time. If a behavior has not been discussed and made into a standard, address it now by setting a standard with an appropriate consequence and carry on by monitoring the situation. If discovered behavior is deemed to be a broken standard, discipline according to the *Discipline Plan*. Try not to overreact.

- If a very defiant child earns a second Strike 3 in the same day, follow through with the deterrent again.
- There may be a time when you realize that your deterrent may be too weak or too strong and needs an adjustment. Run this by your spouse and choose a new deterrent, then have a family meeting with your child and implement it the next time your child earns a Strike 3.

Disciplining Your Child During School Hours

With the hustle and bustle of life, parents often get into the habit of "droppin' off and poppin' in" to their child's school. This will have to change as it's crucial for you to have a connection and working relationship with all of your child's teachers, including caretakers, at all times. When you become aware of a problem at school, decide within 24 hours whether you will handle the situation at home or if you will follow up with the school. If not, the problem will likely become more frequent and intense.

> **Parenting Tip:**
> Sometimes the problem lies in the fit of your child with a particular school, especially if your child has learning problems. If this is the case, you may want to explore alternative schools or opportunities to find a better fit.

If the school calls and says that your child is behaving disrespectfully or with any other negative report (behavioral or academic), stop what you are doing and address it. Start by getting yourself calm. Tell the teacher or administrator that you are trying something new and that you want to work with them. When your child gets home, have a cool, rational conversation about what transpired and discuss ways he might be able to change his behavior. Start by asking questions. Dig in with "who, what, when, and why" questions, if your child's school performance is a problem.

Schools usually deliver discipline of their own and this may be sufficient if the disobedience or disrespect occurs at school. But if the disobedience or disrespect becomes persistent, you may have to reinforce the school's values and your own by disciplining your child at home, too. This is especially the case if this type of behavior happens more than once in the same week.

It's best to address this at home first with a discussion. For instance, you might say, "I want to encourage you to be respectful to your teachers and do what they say. That is the right thing to do." Let him know firmly that if he remains disruptive and defiant, you may follow through with a deterrent.

Discipline and School Work

If your child refuses to do his schoolwork, you need to determine if there's a learning problem before you enforce the Warning, Strike 1, Strike 2, Strike 3 method. Before you discipline for poor academic performance, consider the following guidelines:

- You have realistic expectations and understanding as to <u>what</u> and <u>how much</u> your child should be able to handle in a given school day.
- You have a realistic view of what your child with a learning disorder, if applicable, is capable of. For example a "D" in Social Studies may be the best your child can do if they have dyslexia and dysgraphia. A "D" in Math may be the best your child can do if they have dyscalculia.

- Your child knows how to study and plan out his workload. If child does not know how to study and plan, this is an opportunity for you to teach or consult with teachers for assistance.

- There are not too many distractions competing with your child's academics, such as sports, band, dance, etc.

- Your child knows how to organize himself. If he needs help with this, include this in your *Routine Planning*.

- If you determine that your child "can do" but "won't do" the schoolwork, use the Warning, Strike 1, Strike 2, or Strike 3 method.

Chapter Eight

Reward Planning

Character building is the goal, perfection is not.

Now that you have learned the skills of routine and discipline planning in *The Family Check System*, you are now ready for the third and final plan: The Reward Plan. The "fun" part of *The Family Check System* for the child is the Reward Plan. Rewards are the motivating factor for your child and can transform him from disobedient and belligerent to obedient and cooperative. Think of the reward plan as an act of *good will*. It's not a plan you "have" to do. You are going to do it in an act of generosity and in good faith that your child will participate and make an effort to improve his behaviors. When a parent follows through with this plan, it can balance out the other two plans that may be more intense for the child.

Reward Plan Guidelines

- Even if your child gets a consequence along the way, give a check if he completes his routine in a timely fashion.

- Never take away a check once your child has earned it. Parents commonly make this error. Don't! Follow your *Discipline Plan* if he is disobeying a routine or otherwise disrespecting your authority.

- The parent checks that the child has complied with his routine and if he agrees, the parent will authorize a check to be recorded on *Reward Plan* template. The child will be directed at this time to place this earned check on his *Reward Plan* template. The *Reward Plan* template will be best placed in a central location like your kitchen. This placing of *The Family Check System* will help all involved to be accountable for their individual roles in creating and then keeping the peace in your homes.

- One check per box.

> **PARENTING TIP:**
> Laminate *Reward Plan* for easy weekly use.

REWARD PLANS

There are five types of Reward Plans. Your child will earn checks for his obedient, respectful, and cooperative behaviors including the completion of his AM/PM Routines. Choose plan based on:

- Age and developmental maturity of child
- Number of problematic settings
- Type of rewards
- How often rewards are given

REWARD PLAN 1: For three- to six-year-olds (and young seven-year-olds).

- For behavior in one or more locations (home, school, or grandparent's house).
- Privilege- and toy-based.
- Reward every two days, with option to hold out for a more desirous reward after four days.

> **PARENTING TIP:**
> Give your three- to six-year-old child seven to eight checks daily. At this age, it is crucial to reinforce positive behaviors frequently. And remember to get excited about his accomplishments, and he, too, will get excited.

_____'s
REWARD PLAN 1

15 Checks

30 Checks

As you can see, there are two tiers of rewards for *Reward Plan* 1—one for 15 checks and one for 30.

15 CHECK REWARD

Something the child will enjoy doing versus a "present" that costs money. Examples include:

- Fifteen extra minutes of TV or video time, if applicable
- An extra board game or time with the parents (30 minutes of extra "Daddy time" or extra "Mommy time" to play)

- Help Mom bake a cake or make cookies
- Go to the park
- Go fishing
- Go to the gym
- _____ (Fill in the blank)

> **PARENTING TIP:**
> Families need to be able to cooperate enough to be able to do things together in a timely fashion.

30 CHECK REWARD

A 30-check reward involves more enticing rewards, which makes earning 30 checks more motivating. The idea is not to spend too much money but to dote a little more while not doing anything extravagant that would spoil the child. This will help teach your child to delay gratification. To get to a 30-check reward, he has the option to "roll over his 15 checks" earned over a two-day period and go for a 30-check reward over a four-day period. Examples include:

- Going out for ice cream
- A movie (for the family)
- Getting your nails done
- Going to the motorcycle store or building supply store with Dad
- Going to special events such as favorite football game, opera, ballet, or hunting trip
- _____ (Fill in the blank)

Reward Planning

> **PARENTING TIP:**
> Special events are just that—special. Frame them so your child will be grateful for these things instead of expecting these "extras" as an entitlement. Remind him, no matter your financial situation, that "Money does not grow on trees." Also, always follow through or you won't build trust.

TIPS FOR IMPLEMENTING *REWARD PLAN* 1 SUCCESSFULLY

- Give your child seven to eight "checks" daily and consistently. You can award checks for:
    ⇒ Cooperating with his AM Routine. If this has been a stressful part of your day, offer him "double checks" for cooperating and make this exciting. This is especially necessary with the three- to six-year-olds. Build up the fact that he will get 2 checks for obeying in the morning.
    ⇒ Cooperating with his PM Routine. This can be a "double check" opportunity, too, if he is challenging during the evening time.
    ⇒ Any of the following when you catch your child behaving:
    a) Being polite, sweet, and nice
    b) Being kind to an animal or sibling
    c) Obeying one of your commands quickly or obeying a grandparent
    d) Following directions at school
    e) Being respectful as in saying "Yes, ma'am, yes, sir,"
    f) Doing his routine on time
    g) Initiating hugs and kisses
    h) ____ (Fill in the blank)

Q&A

What do I do if my child gives himself more checks than he deserves, he tears up the template, or erases checks?
You may have to keep up with the *Reward Plan* 1 template by keeping it in a notebook or folder that you personally keep up with versus hanging it on the fridge. These types of behaviors usually occur more with seven and ups than with the three to sixers.

For how long do I apply the *Reward Plan* 1?
Until you have the amount of peace you are looking for and are ready to upgrade to another *Reward Plan*.

What if I can't deliver the reward exactly at the time that he earns it?
Communicate with your child that you will allow him to receive his reward within 24 hours or by the next night.

What if I feel he can delay getting his reward?
It's time to go to *Reward Plan* 2.

REWARD PLAN 2: For more mature four- to six-year-olds (and young seven-year-olds).

- Advanced privilege- and toy-based plan for when *Reward Plan* 1 becomes too easy.
- For behavior in one or more than one location such as the home and/or school.
- Reward on a weekly basis. You can use the same rewards as for *Reward Plan* 1 if they are still motivational. If not, spruce up the rewards.
- Designed to challenge your child to have self-control and to learn delayed gratification.

_____'s

PRIVILEGE-BASED REWARD PLAN 2

Goals:
- Obey Mom, Dad, and teachers quickly.
-

Checks For	SUN	MON	TUE	WED	TH	FRI	SAT	TOTAL
AM Routine								
School								
PM Routine								

_____ **Total Possible Checks**
_____ **Checks Needed for Reward**
_____ **Checks Earned**
_____ **Reward Earned?**

Tips For Implementing *Reward Plan* 2 Successfully

- Explain to your child the number of checks he needs to earn a reward. Make this around 90%. For instance, if the "Total Possible Checks" is 21, tell him that he must earn 19 checks for the week to earn a reward.
- If problematic behavior occurs only at home, mark "X" or place a dash in boxes for School.
- Identify the day to deliver the reward. Saturdays and Sundays are common.

REWARD PLAN 3: Monetary (commission-based) reward for seven- to seventeen-year-olds (and mature six-year-olds) in one location.

- Each check earned has a monetary value called a commission.
- As with all plans, there are opportunities for checks for cooperating and following the AM/PM Routines.
- Total commission paid on a weekly basis.
- Cut back on the things you would normally buy for them like fast food, toys, gas, money for dates and movies (for older kids), etc.

_____'s
COMMISSION-BASED REWARD PLAN 3
$ _____ PER CHECK

Goals:
- Obey Mom, Dad, and teachers quickly.
-

Checks For	SUN	MON	TUE	WED	TH	FRI	SAT	TOTAL
AM Routine								
PM Routine								
Fines								

Total Commission Earned for the Week: _____

Tips for Implementing *Reward Plan* 3 Successfully

- Use a "fine" as a tool to teach polite and refined behavior if you wish. Fines can be valued the same as the check or half the value; you choose. Use of the fine is not mandatory but can be very useful. Do not get the use of the fine confused with the purpose of the Warning, Strike 1, Strike 2, or Strike 3. Fines can be used to help teach better habits while the Warning, Strike 1, Strike 2, or Strike 3 method is for obedience and respect. Some examples of behavior you may fine include immodest, crude, and impolite behaviors.

- On Pay Day, have your child add up the number of checks, minus the number of fines and put the "Total Commission Earned" figure on the designated line. This will help and build self-esteem.

- For Holidays, you may want to announce that "There will be no commissions this week" because things will be more relaxed.

- Some kids don't ask for their commission in an effort to seek the parent's attention. Explore their reasoning if this happens and try to figure out why. Some kids will stop asking for their check and start asking you to spend money on them at convenient stores, fast-food restaurants, and thrifty stores. Stick to the plan of having them ask for their checks and pay for some of these products themselves. Being responsible for obtaining commissions and making small purchases will help promote independence.

> **Parenting Tip:**
> Follow through on paying the commissions when you say you will pay them. If you say you will pay them every Saturday, make sure you do or the system will lose its effectiveness.

Q&A

What is a good rule of thumb for choosing an amount?
The amount is whatever will motivate your child and is in your budget. I suggest a range between 15 cents and $2.50 per check, depending on his age.

How do I know if this system is working?
If your child is getting most of his checks, the system is working.

When is the best time to pay the commissions to the child and how often?
Saturdays and Sundays are the most popular times to settle any and all commissions earned. If the *Reward Plan* ends on a Saturday, Saturday will be a great time to settle. Sunday morning seems to be a good time also. The idea is to pay commission on Saturday or by Sunday midday especially during a school routine because your Sunday PM—Friday AM schedule begins Sunday evening. You will want to have this responsibility as a parent completed by this time so you can get your troops ready to begin the week strong.

REWARD PLAN 4

The same as *Reward Plan* 3 except it involves your child's behavior in two locations, home and school.

_____'s

COMMISSION-BASED REWARD PLAN 4

$ _____ PER CHECK

Goals:

- Obey Mom, Dad, and teachers quickly.
-

CHECKS FOR	SUN	MON	TUE	WED	TH	FRI	SAT	TOTAL
AM ROUTINE								
SCHOOL								
PM ROUTINE								
FINES								

Total Commission Earned for the Week: _____

REWARD PLAN 5

Similar to *Reward Plan 2* in that it is privilege based.

- Plan is for **seven- to seventeen-year-olds.**
- For a parent who does not want to give his child a commission-based reward.
- Earn checks daily by cooperating with and completing AM/PM routines.
- For disobedient and disrespectful behavior in one or two settings.
- Consider rewards such as extended privileges on weekends like later bedtimes, staying at a friend's house or outing longer, extended electronic time, etc.

_____'s
PRIVILEGE-BASED REWARD PLAN 5
For Obedient and Cooperative Behavior at Home and at School

Goals:
- Obey Mom, Dad, and teachers quickly.
-

Checks For	Sun	Mon	Tue	Wed	Th	Fri	Sat	TOTAL
AM Routine								
School								
PM Routine								

_____ Total Possible Checks
_____ Checks Needed for Reward
_____ Checks Earned

Tips for Implementing *Reward Plan 5* Successfully

- Explain to your child the number of checks he needs to earn a reward. Make this around 90%. For instance, if the "Total Possible Checks" is 21, tell him that he must earn 19 checks for the week to earn a reward.
- If problematic behavior occurs only at home, mark an "X" or place a dash in boxes for school.
- Identify a day to deliver the reward. Saturdays and Sundays are common.

CONCLUSION

It is now time to lead your family journey from chaos to peace. My fellow parent, please do not believe the excuse "It's too late to impart my rules and values! My child is almost of age." Consider using *The Family Check System* until the day your young adult "leaves the nest." If your child is under 18 years old and living under your roof, you still have time to set expectations, standards, and consequences for your soon-to-be legally-aged young adult. You have taken the time to learn some new ways to establish and maintain peace. Keep this commitment to peace and to your child until he is ready to become more independent by moving out and getting his first place away from home.

You still have time to a make a real effort at establishing a right relationship with your child rooted in respect with trust as your primary goal. As long as your older teenager is showing you some respect and willingness to work with you, continue to teach him, never give up on him. Don't give up on your own personal growth as a person, either. You can learn to be more patient, kind, empathetic, etc. Continue to set goals and limits, and follow through with consequences as long as your child will allow you to and as long as necessary.

Once you get *The Family Check System* together, you will have one strong and insightful plan that will train your child to be a young man or young lady of good character and are on your journey to peace in your home. Mutual respect, cooperation, and trust are the goals. Stay strong. Stay firm. Be humble. Stay consistent. Stay involved. You can do this!

APPENDIX

More Examples of Standards and Suggested Consequences

Standards Options	Suggested Consequences
Mild behaviors:	
No play touching or scaring	Warning, Strike 1, Strike 2, or Strike 3
Snacks should be at least 45 minutes before mealtime	Warning, Strike 1, Strike 2, or Strike 3 OR Fine
No shoes on furniture	Warning, Strike 1, Strike 2, or Strike 3 OR Fine
Finish lawn care and do a good job	Warning, Strike 1, Strike 2, or Strike 3 OR Fine
Children must ask permission from parents before leaving a family meeting	Warning, Strike 1, Strike 2, or Strike 3
Eating must be limited to kitchen area unless otherwise approved	Warning, Strike 1, Strike 2, or Strike 3 or Fine (Parent chooses at time of infraction)
Be polite and considerate, no crude behavior or excessive noise in the presence of others	Warning, Strike 1, Strike 2, or Strike 3 OR Time Out OR Fine (if you choose Reward Plan 3 or 4)

Standards Options (continued)	Suggested Consequences (continued)
Wait your turn to speak; no interrupting	Warning, Strike 1, Strike 2, or Strike 3 OR Time Out (parent to choose at time of infraction)
Siblings: Be kind and loving toward each other: no inflaming, arguing, taunting, name calling, being selfish, self-centered, etc.	Warning, Strike 1, Strike 2, or Strike 3 OR Time Out (parent to choose at time of infraction)
Place electronic device on cabinet by 8:30 p.m..	Warning, Strike 1, Strike 2, or Strike 3 or Fine
Be responsible with schoolwork and chores; have pride in schoolwork and learning (No laziness)	Extra chore OR extra educational task
Be polite by showing good manners at the table and be considerate by picking up after self	Warning, Strike 1, Strike 2, or Strike 3 OR Fine (if you choose *Reward Plan* 3 or 4)
Responsibilities are a priority; therefore, no electronics until schoolwork is complete for the day and you have permission	Warning, Strike 1, Strike 2, or Strike 3

Standards Options (continued)	Suggested Consequences (continued)
Moderate behaviors:	
No sitting on, tackling, or body-slamming people	Warning, Strike 1, Strike 2, or Strike 3 OR Automatic Deterrent (parent to choose)
No behavior problems at school	May be Automatic Deterrent
Turn in all assignments: No zeros	Automatic Deterrent
Be respectful to property (toys, telephones, etc. No destruction, don't be too rough)	Pay for damage or do extra chore; acknowledgment of wrong doing
No use of the internet unless supervised by parent	Warning, Strike 1, Strike 2, or Strike 3 OR Automatic Deterrent
Severe behaviors:	
No hitting, kicking, spitting, biting, etc.	Automatic Deterrent
Abstain from use of alcohol, drugs, tobacco, leaving home without permission, sexual relations, violence	Automatic Deterrent or get police involved, if necessary

STANDARDS OPTIONS (continued)	SUGGESTED CONSEQUENCES (continued)
Tell the whole truth: No omissions, no spinning, or part truths, manipulations, no lying, cheating, stealing	Automatic Deterrent
No contact with people through devices unless parents approve. Kids are responsible for letting parents know of any loopholes	Automatic Deterrent

NOTES

NOTES

CPSIA information can be obtained at www.ICGtesting.com
Printed in the USA
LVOW04s2006110914

403574LV00003B/3/P